THE ONLY
WOMAN
IN THE ROOM

QUOTES AND WISDOM FOR
A FEARLESS LIFE

Annette Merritt Cummings, M.B.A.

WESTBOW
PRESS®
A DIVISION OF THOMAS NELSON
& ZONDERVAN

Scripture taken from the King James Version of the Bible (https://www.biblegateway.com/versions/King-James-Version-KJV-Bible/#copy)

WestBow Press books may be ordered through booksellers or by contacting:

WestBow Press
A Division of Thomas Nelson & Zondervan
1663 Liberty Drive
Bloomington, IN 47403
www.westbowpress.com
1 (866) 928-1240

Because of the dynamic nature of the Internet, any web addresses or links contained in this book may have changed since publication and may no longer be valid. The views expressed in this work are solely those of the author and do not necessarily reflect the views of the publisher, and the publisher hereby disclaims any responsibility for them.

Any people depicted in stock imagery provided by Thinkstock are models, and such images are being used for illustrative purposes only. Certain stock imagery © Thinkstock.

ISBN: 978-1-5127-7505-1 (sc)
ISBN: 978-1-5127-7506-8 (hc)
ISBN: 978-1-5127-7504-4 (e)

Library of Congress Control Number: 2017902128

Print information available on the last page.

WestBow Press rev. date: 04/10/2017

CONTENTS

Dedication and Thanks

My life and career have made for an amazing and rewarding journey. I could not have made it without my mother, Virgie Nell Matthews Merritt Dowdell, brothers, LaDon and William, grandparents, Laura A. and Henry Merritt, our children, Michael, Angela and Tahlia. And the prayers of all.

Iran, my husband of thirty-one years, encouraged, supported and nudged me to write this book. For that and much more, thank you.

But they that wait upon the Lord
Shall renew their strength.

They shall mount up
With wings as eagles.

They shall run,
And not be weary.

They shall walk,
And not be faint.

—Isaiah 40:31 (KJV),
8th Century BC,
Hebrew Prophet

My favorite Bible verse.
I spent twelve years as a "diversity road warrior," literally on the road most of the time, working as a consultant, speaker and diversity trainer. I kept this Bible verse framed on my desk and read it at least once a week, to give me strength and insight.

My faith in the power of this particular verse was confirmed by Joshua DuBois, who served as an informal spiritual advisor to President Barack Obama. When asked what is the one piece of advice he would give to would-be leaders? He said, "Read Isaiah 40:31."

On the 50th Anniversary of the Selma March and Bloody Sunday, President Obama closed his speech with Isaiah 40:31 and said: "when it feels that the road is too hard and the torch is too heavy, we will remember these early travelers and draw strength from their example and hold firmly to the words of the prophet Isaiah."

INTRODUCTION

The right words at the right time, can move and inspire all of us. I am sure that anyone who aspires to be a writer collects quotes and every professional speaker looks for exactly the right quote to make a point or leave a lasting impression on the audience. In that spirit, I offer this book of inspirational quotations along with the highlights of my career and life's journey. I used these hymns, bible verses and quotes to propel my career, starting out in a temp job at the Internal Revenue Service, as a receptionist. I finished my career as the Vice President and National Director of Diversity Services with one of the world's largest ad agencies, Omnicom (Bernard Hodes Group). These quotations, words of wisdom, poems, bible verses and thoughts have inspired me and illuminated my life: from unwed mother at seventeen to *summa cum laude* college graduate at age thirty.

After college, I began my career as a public relations executive, then an advertising manager, corporate secretary and fundraising/ development executive, public relations agency vice president and finally as a consultant, speaker and trainer. I had the opportunity to work with some of the major institutions and Fortune 500 corporations in America.

Many of the quotes and poems included in this book, I have used in my speeches and workshops to illustrate a point and engage the audience. Other quotations are my private guideposts, acquired over my lifetime to keep me inspired, moving forward and to check my attitude.

Some quotes have been contributed by my darling husband of over thirty years, Iran Cummings. I thank him for being an avid collector of inspirational words too...no wonder God brought us together. Many quotes have been gleaned from reading, e.g., from histories, biographies, mysteries and historical fiction. At any given time, I am reading at least four books.

> Books: The most effective weapon against
> intolerance and ignorance.
> —Lyndon B. Johnson (1908—1973), 36th President
> of the United States, he signed the Civil Rights Act
> (1964) and the Voting Rights Act of 1965

My disclaimer: I have made every attempt to determine who said what, but sometimes the exact origin of a quote may be lost to history.

Before my "downsized" retirement in July of 2010, I spent twelve years as a speaker, trainer and consultant working on hiring and retaining a diverse workforce, with many organizations. The last couple of years I have given a lot of thought to what I could share that would be helpful to my former colleagues and clients and indeed anyone interested in a better, more diverse world. I opened my diversity workshops with this admonition: you must know the past, to understand the present in order to predict the future.

The past is never dead. It's not even the past.
—William Faulkner (1897—1962), writer,
and Nobel Prize Laureate

Lessons learned as a diversity road warrior

For the last thirty years, America's business and public sector leaders have talked about "walking the talk" around issues of diversity. Many books have been written to guide and help diversity practitioners, consultants, business and government leaders make the leap from "talk" to implementation and the "demystification" of diversity and what makes an inclusive society or organization. Yes, certainly knowledge is power, so make sure you have a solid knowledge base and understanding of cultures, diversity, values and behaviors and know how to lead change in an organization.

Personally, I have found that maintaining your faith in humanity and a commitment to change allows you to continue the work, despite barriers and resistance. These factors are critical to success and to your own well-being.

I hope the quotes we have gathered will serve as guideposts and that my personal story will inspire and arm you to complete your own particular journey with passion and joy.

MY LIFE JOURNEY
Be Fearless, Our Family Motto

A Southerner by Birth, Sweet Home Alabama

My very first childhood memory is sitting on the porch swing with my grandmother listening to her read a poem to me. I was born in the Deep South or Black Belt, in 1946, in Crenshaw County, Alabama, about thirty miles, from Montgomery. The all black community, Helicon, was founded by freed slaves, one of which was my great grandfather, Henry W. Merritt (known as Old Man Henry). We were isolated and somewhat insulated from Jim Crow Alabama, in our rural community. We did, of course, have to shop and take care of personal business in the cities near our home: Luverne, Troy and Montgomery, where the water fountains, stores, restaurants were segregated by "White" and "Colored." We lived with my grandparents for a time. My grandmother was a kindergarten and first grade teacher for over forty years (and my first teacher); and my grandfather was a farmer and a respected community leader.

Even though I have traveled far from my "sweet home" Alabama, with its well-water, pecan and chinaberry trees, the smokehouse and yes, outhouse, I still cry when I leave...after every visit. I still remember the red dirt, dusty roads of my childhood and every bend and turn in the road is more familiar to me than any place I have lived since that long ago time.

My brother (William), grandfather (Pa Henry), grandmother (Mamma Laura), me, Aunt Sylvia, and oldest brother (Erbia LaDon). Around 1949, in Helicon, Alabama, in their farmhouse (regrettably burned down now).

My father, Henry W. Merritt, served as an ambulance driver during World War II in France. My mother, Virgie Nell Dowdell, was and still is a beautiful, now ninety-three years-old, mother and hard-working daughter of the South. They moved to Detroit and then later to Cleveland, OH. My parents, like many black parents after World War II, left the Jim Crow South and their children, in the care of their grandparents, while they moved north to find a better life, sometimes those children stayed for the summer, sometimes for years at a time.

Forced to grow up

I left Alabama permanently in 1956, at age nine, and moved to Cleveland with my mother, father and brothers, after my beloved Aunt Sylvia, a ninth grade English teacher, was burned before my eyes. Her night gown caught fire as she was starting a fire with kerosene in a wood stove in our shared front bedroom. I had watched her do this many times. After they put her in a car to take her to the hospital in Montgomery, thirty agonizing miles away, I was not allowed to visit because of my age. I never saw her again, until her heart-breaking funeral.

I was fourteen years old before I could strike a match and sixteen before I no longer smelled burning flesh in that front bedroom every time I visited my grandparents. Now, at the age of seventy, I mostly remember the good times with my playmates, Betty and Grace, cousins, Earlie Mae and Lucille, my Aunt Sylvia and Uncle Little Buddy, Mamma Laura and Pa Henry. My brothers and I spent many happy years, embraced in the loving arms of our small, black farming community with one red dirt road running through it and with little exposure to white America.

My parents divorced when I was fourteen. I attended Cleveland Public Schools, from fifth grade through Cuyahoga Community College. *All* school buildings where I attended elementary, junior high and high school have been demolished.

In 1977, I received a B.A. *summa cum laude*, from Cleveland State University. My high school study, at East Technical High School, was cut short by my out-of-wedlock pregnancy in the eleventh grade, at age sixteen. In those days, the pregnant female student had to leave school, friends and classmates. The expectant father was allowed to stay in school and go to the prom. My beautiful baby boy, Michael, my Mother and brother, William and I lived in a studio apartment with a Murphy bed, couch and a crib. Even though it was tough, my Mom-a-dear would not let me accept food stamps.

I was pregnant again (I know!) when I married the father (Bennie Jones) of my wonderful children, Michael and Angela Jones, in 1964. We grew up and apart, and divorced in 1974.

Education through perseverance

All my degrees, including my high school diploma (John Hay Extension High School) were earned through part-time or night school attendance. Since I was in the advanced studies program at East Tech, I was able to have two babies (Michael-1963, Angela-1964) and still finish school by age nineteen. From 1969 to 1977, I spent every summer attending college.

My first job, after my children were both walking and potty trained, was with the Internal Revenue Service, as a receptionist, a temporary job. In my opinion, the receptionist is one of the most critical positions in an organization, yet is hugely undervalued and underpaid. Before my temporary assignment was completed, I was hired as a clerk-typist, a permanent Federal employee, with the Department of Defense at the Armed Forces Entrance and Examining Station (AFEES). This was during the Vietnam War and I was the only woman in administration. Given the turmoil of that time, even a clerk-typist felt the stress of the war. We had a bomb threat, it seemed, about every other week and had to evacuate the building. Our offices were highly visible, right off Public Square in downtown Cleveland. The staff was made up of personnel from all the armed services, Army, Navy (commanding officer), Marines and Air Force. I was the personnel clerk for the regular Army personnel assigned to AFEES and also served as an escort for the physicals for volunteer nurses. I so admired the regular Army soldiers for their willingness to repeatedly volunteer for duty in Vietnam, while others were doing as much as was legal (sometimes illegal) to avoid service.

One of my best decisions was to take a stenography/speed writing course in 1968, so I could qualify for a higher grade level in the Federal government. I met my best friend of forty-eight years, Connie Jones, in that class. She mentioned that DuPont was looking for a stenographer to work in their steno pool. This was the beginning of Affirmative Action by corporate America, so they were specifically looking for an African American. I started in the chemical plant in the Flats area of Cleveland (think, the river that burned!) in February of 1969, where I was the first African American woman and first female in administration who was not related to a current employee. The human resources manager warned me that two other black women had not lasted six weeks, before quitting. Initially, the white stenographers would not use the bathroom immediately after me or take breaks with me. I didn't care, it was more money than I had ever made or dreamed that I would make. A number of these same women, became my friends. I danced the polka at many a Polish wedding.

The only woman in the plant

Later I became the first woman, in almost 100 years of operation, to work down in the plant, as a production clerk, rather than in the traditional jobs in the office/admin buildings on the hill. I was incredibly excited about this challenge. My move down the hill into production was quite controversial with the other female employees and the all-male production team. I had my own office adjacent to the department supervisor. I had never heard so much cursing in my life. The men were testing me, to see what I would do or say. I took it and picked my moments to engage in the joking banter that is a part of blue-collar, mostly male environments. I suspect that the reason my supervisor, Steve Gerow, a chemical engineer, became one of my mentors was because of my performance under stress. The hourly guys did finally accept me and treated me with respect in the end.

The value of a union shop is that all open jobs were posted and if it meant a raise, I would bid on the job, many women followed me into the plant. I moved from stenographer to payroll clerk, production clerk, truck dispatcher, and shipping clerk and was eventually elected as a local union steward with the Chemical Workers of America.

My participation in the union/management negotiations was a valuable lesson. Although the union president warned me that "once black folks are hired, many of the perks and benefits will go away," such as company picnics, Christmas parties and hiring of family members. I argued vehemently with him.

He was right.

No person is your friend who demands your silence; or denies your right to grow.

—Alice Walker (b. 1944),
African-American writer and novelist,
and wrote The Color Purple

My career as a communications professional begins

DuPont paid for my education, through tuition reimbursement. I graduated from Cuyahoga Community College, (A.A. with honors—business major, 1975) and Cleveland State University, B.A. (1977) a communications major, with a minor in marketing, *summa cum laude.* With my mind firmly fixed on the future, I risked all, by taking a six month leave of absence (took nineteen credit hours for two quarters straight) with no guarantee of a job with DuPont when I finished.

After graduation, I was hired as an advertising and sales promotion representative at DuPont corporate in Wilmington, Delaware; and I was the first African American woman to hold that position. That opportunity would never have happened without my shipping office supervisor, Tom Woods, advocating on my behalf, with corporate human resources staff. I eventually interviewed in Wilmington with the Corporate Giving and Advertising departments. All my trip expenses were covered, including my stay at the Hotel du Pont. I received an offer from both departments, and because I knew so little about philanthropy at the time, I accepted the offer from the Advertising Department. My children and I moved to a new townhouse in a suburb of Wilmington, DE. After only one year, Michael returned to Warrensville Hts., Ohio to live with his Dad. The one good thing he got out of that move was he learned how to skateboard and was really good at it. In Wilmington, he was one of only two black boys in the junior high school and both of them were on the basketball team. Despite his talent, we had to fight (constantly) with the coach to get him playing time. This was Michael's first real encounter with prejudice and he learned how to navigate in a majority white environment. I worked for E.I. du Pont de Nemours & Company for over twelve years, long enough to be vested in the pension plan.

Move to Motown changes my life

In 1982, I moved to Detroit with my daughter, Angela. I was offered a job by my former supervisor, Steve Gerow, as a Technical Sales Representative (*the only woman, only black person, and only sales person without a technical education*) with Parker Chemical, a division of Occidental Petroleum. They gave me a crash course in metallurgy and in plating chemicals. I was one of a hundred sales reps. My clients were the supervisors and engineers in the "dirty" part of the automobile factories, where they cleaned the metals. While I loved my customers, this job was not for me. I do know that I opened the door for other women and people of color.

Despite our best selves, we all get discouraged at times, doubt our ability and listen to those negative voices. During those times, we should call on our inner resources and seek spiritual guidance to inspire us to keep on keeping on. I briefly worked for myself and partnered in a solar-energy business. We were ahead of our time!

Grab the broom of anger and drive off the beast of fear.

—Zora Neale Hurston (1891—1960),
Folklorist and writer,
wrote about African Americans and
their culture in the rural South,
and was a part of the Harlem Renaissance

The best jobs or opportunities come unexpectedly and through the goodwill of others. We must make the most of our alliances and seek mentors with all who are willing. I urge women and people of color to keep an open mind when selecting mentors...a number of mine have been white men. See Chapter 9, *Gratitude.*

It was not an easy decision to get a divorce, move out-of-state, or take a job in a technical field and in sales—a rather drastic shift in my career. But it surely paid off, professionally and personally.

I met my husband, Iran Cummings (or rather I found him under the Christmas tree) in Detroit, at a tree trimming party in 1983. Coincidentally we were both transplants from Cleveland, OH. We married in 1985, I gained a six-year old, stepdaughter, Tahlia, who lived mostly with her mother Janice (now deceased) in Cleveland, until age fourteen, while he gained two teenagers. In total, Iran lived in Detroit for seventeen years, I lived there for fourteen years. I still love Detroit and the Midwest. The "rest of the story" is in Chapter 8, *My Career Journey: the Only Woman in the Room.*

Our wedding in 1985,
Annette with Michael (son)

Iran and Annette cutting the cake.

Time is the coin of your life.
You spend it.
Do not allow others to spend it for you.

—Carl Sandburg (1878—1967),
poet, writer and editor,
and he was awarded three Pulitzer Prizes

One of his Pulitzer Prizes was for his biography of Abraham Lincoln and the first of many biographies I have read about our American presidents. I visited the Carl Sandburg Home National Historic Site, in Flat Rock, NC when we had a second home in Laurel Park, NC. I also had the privilege of leading a diversity and inclusion seminar for the National Park Rangers and staff. Sandberg had books in every nook, shelf and space (me too) and also, proudly displayed an award from the NAACP.

Replenish Your Soul from Time to Time

The quotes, poems, and hymns, I have selected to share in this book have inspired me throughout my life and career. The sections speak to my journey and the necessary life skills needed to attain your goals.

- A willingness to change and be courageous
- The importance of perseverance and the value of education
- The role of faith
- How commitment is essential to success
- Diversity and inclusion in our lives and in America
- The healing power of humor
- Gratitude as a way of moving through life with purpose
- Finally, a few parting words and lessons

My hope is that others will be inspired to pursue their dreams, no matter the naysayers or obstacles they will face. After my divorce and struggle as a single mother in the workforce, I adopted a motto: if you are not for me, you are against me. That served as a way to determine how I would spend my time and with whom. Now, it sounds a bit extreme in hindsight, but it was what I needed at the time to stay focused and not be distracted or give in to discouragement from the nay-sayers.

Two regrets in my career decisions: One—I should have accepted the part-time job offer from the local ABC television station while in college; and I also should have tried harder to find a baby-sitter. Two—I should have gone to law school, when I was accepted—twice (Temple University and the University of Louisville). However, I am grateful for how my career, my life and my children's lives turned out and would *not* change anything.

My advice: find your passion, keep focus on the good that people do, have a commitment to excellence, hold your family and friends close, and you will be successful and at peace.

Chapter 1.

CHANGE

Not everything that is faced can be changed,
but nothing can be changed until it is faced.

—James Baldwin (1924—1987),
African-American essayist and novelist

My inheritance: $1.00

My father told me I had ruined my life because I was sixteen and pregnant. He insisted, by yelling at me, that I would never be anything.

If you can imagine what that does to a young woman, scared enough already. Fortunately, my dear mother stood by me. My "Mom-a-dear" provided financial and emotional support for me when I was lost, confused and disappointed in myself. Although, she was separated from my father, she went back to him thinking he would be a help to us. Surprise, "when someone shows you who they are, believe them." (Maya Angelou)

My feelings about this time in my life are perfectly captured by the song "Piece by Piece," by Kelly Clarkson. Her relationship with her father is shared by so many. I am thankful to know men, like my husband, my ex and my son, who do love and care for their daughters and indeed all their children. A father's relationship with his daughter/s allows us to figure out what kind of man we want and need. Some men, indeed too many, fail the test of fatherhood.

My father left my brothers and I, exactly—one dollar—in his will, to keep us from breaking the will, thus depriving us of land that had been in our family for three generations. My brother, William, has gradually bought the land back, praise God.

I read *The Power of Positive Thinking* in 1974 and it changed my life. Dr. Peale's techniques are criticized by some, but I am a believer...

Change your thoughts and you change your world.
—Dr. Norman Vincent Peale (1898—1993),
author and motivational speaker,
and he wrote *The Power of Positive Thinking*

A New Day

This is the beginning of a new day.
God has given me this day to use as I will.

When tomorrow comes, this day will be gone forever,
leaving in its place something that I have traded for it.

I want it to be gain, and not loss, good and not evil,
success and not failure; in order that I shall not regret
the price that I have paid for it.

—Unknown

"A New Day" has sustained my husband and me for the last five years, and continues to remind us to make the most of our gifts and blessings each day. We have the full poem on the wall in our guest bathroom, so we see it many times a day. If you want to keep focused on the ideas that are important to you, read and reread them often.

Excuses are the nails that build the house of failure...
no excuses.

—Motto of Central Catholic High School
Football Team, Cleveland OH

My grandchildren, Corey and Courtney Jones, Angela's children,
graduated from Central Catholic. And now we can proudly declare
that they are both college graduates: Corey, from Bowling Green
University and Courtney, from Wright State University (BA) and
Union College (MA). Donte and Trevor are Michael's two sons,
both are pursuing their careers in Grand Rapids and in Cleveland
Hts., OH.

A hundred times a day I remind myself that my inner and outer life are based on the labors of other men, living and dead, and that I must exert myself in order to give in the same measure as I have received and am still receiving.

—Albert Einstein (1879—1955), German-American, physicist, and awarded the Nobel Prize for Physics in 1921

I have to constantly remind myself that my life has been enhanced by the "labors and sacrifices" of others. Some are living and many are dead. This reflection helps me to go on and push myself to honor those sacrifices.

Einstein was a civil rights activist. In a speech in 1946, at Lincoln University, he called racism "a disease of white people." For more information on his activism in Princeton, NJ, read: *Einstein on Race and Racism*, by Jerome and Taylor, (Rutgers University Press, 2006).

If you take too long in deciding what to do with your life, you'll find you've already done it.

—George Bernard Shaw (1856—1950)
Irish dramatist and critic. Author of Pygmalion (1913),
which became the musical, *"My Fair Lady"*

One of the key inspirations in life is music. *My Fair Lady*, is one of my favorite musicals and film. Yes, I love the songs and the story, but I particularly like the idea that with education you can change your life for the better.

Broadway musicals are so uplifting and mostly joyful. I can't wait to see *"Hamilton,"* and of course I have the cast recording. *The Sound of Music* is another movie I can watch over and over again, and have. *"My Favorite Things,"* sung by Julie Andrews, is my ringtone.

The Serenity Prayer

God grant me the serenity to accept the things I cannot change;
Courage to change the things I can; and wisdom to know the difference.

Trusting that He will make all things right if I surrender to His Will;
That I may be reasonably happy in this life and supremely happy with Him
Forever in the next. Amen.

—Reinhold Niebuhr (1892—1971),
American Protestant theologian

I have kept the first verse of this prayer on my desk or in my kitchen since 1975; and it helped me get through a divorce, and all the many abrupt changes and struggles we all face in this life. This is the Alcoholics Anonymous prayer for people struggling with addiction.

Chapter 2.

TRUTH AND COURAGE

Wisdom is the reward you get for a lifetime of
listening when you'd have preferred to talk.

—Doug Larson (b.1926),
columnist and editor

Our deepest fear is not that we are inadequate.
Our deepest fear is that we are powerful beyond
measure.
It is our light, not our darkness, that most frightens us.

We ask ourselves, who am I to be brilliant, gorgeous,
talented, fabulous?
Actually, who are you not to be? You are a child of God.

And as we let our own light shine, we unconsciously
give other people permission to do the same. As
we're liberated from our own fear, our presence
automatically liberates others.

From the book: *A Return to Love.*
—Marianne Williamson (Born 1952),
spiritual teacher, author, and lecturer

*Often attributed to Nelson Mandela. Williamson's not sure how
attribution was given to Mandela, but said: "No, Mandela did not
quote me, but I would be honored if he did."

Our family motto is derived from this poem: "be fearless." I first
used it as my email signature, then my daughter, Angela picked it
up and then my grandchildren: my grandson, Corey "Bapes" Jones,
a Cleveland rapper, has it tattooed on his arm. I'm not yet ready to
go that far; but who knows, I just might.

It takes a lot of courage to show your dreams to someone else.

—Erma Bombeck (1927—1996),
humorist, columnist, from 1965 to 1996,
and she wrote over 4,000 newspaper columns and fifteen books

As a fellow Ohioan and avid newspaper reader, I believe I read every column she wrote in the Cleveland Plain Dealer. Bombeck spoke directly to the women and wives in transition, during the 70's and 80's. She was an excellent writer and humorist, much admired.

You gain strength, courage and confidence by every experience which you must stop and look fear in the face...you must do the thing you think you cannot do.

—Eleanor Roosevelt (1894—1962),
First Lady, 1933-45, Wife of Franklin D. Roosevelt,
32nd President of U.S.,
and United Nations Diplomat

Courage, ethical behavior and truth-telling are required in order to live a life that you can be proud of the "living," during your career and later in life.

The way to right wrongs is to turn
the light of truth upon them.

—Ida B. Wells-Barnett (1862—1931),
African American journalist and anti-lynching crusader,
active in the suffrage movement,
and she founded the first Black women's suffrage group in Chicago

Recommended reading:
Blood at the Root, a Racial Cleansing in America, by Patrick Phillips. In 1912, whites drove out the entire black population of Forsyth County, GA. The author lived in Forsyth County as a child and decided to investigate the story and the myth surrounding this "white riot."

Labor Day differs in every essential way from the other holidays of the year in any country. All other holidays are, in more or less degree, connected with conflicts and battles of man's prowess over man, of strife and discord for greed and power, of glories achieved by one nation over another. Labor Day is devoted to no man, living or dead, to no sect, race or nation.

—Samuel Gompers (1850—1924),
founder and president of the American Federation of Labor

One of the great learning experiences for me, was when I served as a union steward, in the DuPont plant in Cleveland, OH. I learned that the first-line supervisors and managers were secretly delighted when hourly workers received a raise or another benefit, since they would also get a raise and receive the new benefit. Basically, if you must work for a living, we are all in this together.

Remarks at Dr. Martin Luther King Jr. College Preparatory High School graduation, June, 2015, Chicago, IL.

Maybe you have been tested a lot more, and a lot earlier in life than most young people; maybe you have more scars than they do; days when you feel more tired than someone your age should ever really feel. But graduates, tonight I want you to understand that every scar that you have, is not just a reminder that you got hurt, but that you survived.

—Michelle Obama (b.1964),
attorney and first African-American First Lady (2009—2016),
wife of Barack Obama, 44th President of the United States,
and author, *American Grown: The Story of the White House Kitchen Garden and Gardens Across America,* 2012

Hadiya Pendleton was a student and member of King College Prep Class of 2015, and was killed by random gunfire, on January 29, 2013. She was killed a mile from the Obama's home in Chicago, a couple of weeks after she had marched with the school drill team in Obama's 2013 Inaugural Parade. First Lady Michelle Obama attended her funeral.

Of course, I have Michelle's *White House Kitchen Garden* book...the quiche is excellent.

Chapter 3.

PERSERVERANCE AND THE VALUE OF EDUCATION

Success is a function of consistent common sense (more) than it is of genius.

—An Wang (1920—1990),
Chinese American computer engineer,
co-founder of Wang Laboratories

Perhaps some attributes are innate and some are learned. I learned the value of education from my Grandmother Laura A. Merritt and was born with the perseverance of my ancestors, with the ability to overcome and triumph over obstacles. I watched my Mother triumph over many obstacles as a poor, divorced woman of color, with the odds stacked against her and her children. She worked as a cashier and supervisor, in hospital kitchens and school cafeterias and retired at seventy-five from Cleveland Public Schools.

"Education is yours and can't be taken away from you," so it is never too late to acquire more education. You may lose your job but if you continue to add to your credentials, then you have options. I have tried to instill that in my children. I used to call it keeping "a hidden agenda." I could take whatever disappointments or hardships of any job, with any company, as long as I gained additional skills or they paid for my continuing education.

Education remains the key to both
economic and political empowerment.

—Barbara Jordan (1936—1996),
Lawyer, educator and Congressional Representative,
and first African American Congresswoman to
come from the South

A powerful speaker and an inspiration for all who aspire to
move audiences with our words.

Life is going to be difficult, and dreadful things will happen. What you do is to move along, get on with it, and be tough. Not in the sense of being mean to others, but tough with yourself and making a deadly effort not to be defeated.

—Katharine Hepburn (1907—2003),
stage and film actress

I love her movies, particularly, *The Philadelphia Story* and *The Lion in Winter*. She was a model for how to grow old gracefully and still be fully yourself. I highly recommend her autobiography, *Me: Stories of My Life*, 1991.

Annette, in Detroit MI, around 1948.

My father was working for Chrysler and my mother was a waitress. Thirty-three years later, I returned to Detroit, where I met my husband, Iran...coming full-circle.

Perseverance is the key, these words and this picture were on the front of my 50th birthday announcement to friends and relatives. I asked them to help me celebrate my fifty years on earth by making a donation, in lieu of gifts, to a scholarship fund for single mothers, at my alma mater, Cleveland State University.

Cleveland State University

SUMMER 1996

Perspective

Birthday gifts endow scholarship

"Education is a great concern of mine and I just had the desire to give back."

Annette Merritt Cummings

An article about my donation to Cleveland State University, in the alumni publication, *Perspective*, summer, 1986

To teach men how to live without certainty, and yet without being paralyzed by hesitation, is perhaps the chief thing philosophy can still do.

—Albert Schweitzer (1875—1965),
theologian, philosopher, organist,
mission doctor in Africa,
and won 1952 Nobel Peace Prize

The study of philosophy and critical thinking has the power to be life-changing and should be taught in junior high school rather than waiting until college.

Live to learn and you will learn to live.

—Unknown

Education and the ability to think critically are the essential keys to a productive and successful life.

Horace Mann, Antioch University's first president, speaking to the graduating class at Antioch College.

Be ashamed to die until you have won
some victory for humanity.

—Horace Mann (1796—1859),
educator and congressman,
Antioch's founding mission: coeducation and
equal opportunity for Negroes

One accurate measurement is worth a thousand expert opinions.

—Grace Murray Hopper (1906—1992),
mathematician and Rear Admiral in the U.S. Navy,
and pioneer in the development of computer technology

How ironic that Admiral Hooper pioneered computer technology, yet "geeks" are believed to be mostly male. The lack of diversity within many of the tech companies has justifiably come under scrutiny, e.g., women and minorities other than Asian.

Happily *Hidden Figures*, the non-fiction biographical book by Margot Lee Shetterly and the hit movie, tell the story of the decades of contributions of three African-American women (Katherine Johnson, Dorothy Vaughn, and Mary Jackson) to the early years of NASA and the launching of the U.S. Space Shuttle program. So, yes, women and women of color can be "geeks." In 2015, President Barack Obama awarded the Presidential Medal of Freedom to one of the women: Katherine Johnson, a physicist, space scientist, and mathematician.

Some of the blame for the barriers to employment is due to "stereotypical" thinking about who has the necessary skill set and how they go about recruiting for diversity. Most jobs are acquired through who you know, in others words, a referral from an employee. If you don't have a diverse workforce, you will "get what you've already got."

Unless you try to do something beyond what you have already mastered, you will never grow.

—Ralph Waldo Emerson (1803—1882),
lecturer, poet and essayist

Continuing education is not just a program, it is essential to keeping your mind alert and active for your entire life. Since my retirement, I have taken any course I have an interest in and plan to continue as long as I am able.

The Richland County Library System in Columbia, SC, is one of the best library systems I've seen. Courses as diverse as Tai-Chi, how to make sushi, grow roses, and conduct genealogy research, are just a few of the courses I've taken. And I am a proud member of the Thursday Book Club at the Sandhills Branch of Richland County Library. They are a wonderful group of women, mostly white, mostly NOT born in Columbia, SC., and mostly retired.

Chapter 4.

FAITH, PURPOSE AND SPIRITUAL VALUES

The ultimate measure of a man is not
where he stands in moments of comfort
and convenience, but where he stands at
times of challenge and controversy.

—Martin Luther King Jr. (1929—1968),
civil rights leader and clergyman,
and was awarded Nobel Peace Prize, in 1964

Our faith and spiritual values are what sustain us and feed our souls. The gospel performance by Helen Baylor, *"Helen's Testimony: I had a Praying Grandmother,"* has always touched me. I believe our grandmother's faith and prayer are at the heart of our strength and determination and is our true "inheritance."

Jackie Robinson's Tombstone: a life is not important, except in the impact it has on other lives.

—Jackie Robinson (1919—1972),
Hall of Fame baseball player, businessman,
and first black baseball player to play in the
American major leagues, 1947

Hold yourself responsible for a higher standard than anybody else expects of you.

—Henry Ward Beecher (1813—1887),
Congregational minister, abolitionist,
and influential Protestant spokesman

I was raised a Baptist (baptized at age six in Helicon Missionary Baptist Church) but joined the Congregational United Church of Christ in 1975. My reasons: the Shaker Heights UCC had a white female minister (Baptists didn't) and she had seven children. The minister invited those who lived near the church to help revive a dying church and integrate the church. Later on, I discovered that Congregationalists had been leaders in the abolitionist movement, in America and a part of the freeing of the Amistad slaves in New England. I also believe that Sunday morning at 11:00 a.m. should be the most integrated and diverse hour of the week...not the most segregated. We will know that we have an inclusive society when the majority of churches are not separated by race.

My reason for hope: a friend recommended the Bible Study Fellowship (BSF) to me in 2015. Meetings for women are held every Thursday morning at Shannon Baptist Church, Columbia, SC, from September to May. Around three hundred or so women participate; and they are White, Black, Hispanic and Asian. All age groups come regularly, pray together and pray for each other. One of my goals when I retired was to read the whole Bible. I have now made a good start with our study of Revelation and John, next is Romans. BSF is available in most major cities in the U.S.A. and is also international.

Amazing Grace
(Excerpt)

Amazing Grace, how sweet the sound, that saved a wretch like me.
I once was lost but now am found, was blind, but now I see.

When we've been here ten thousand years, bright shining as the sun.
We've no less days to sing God's praise than when we've first begun.

Amazing Grace, how sweet the sound, that saved a wretch like me.
I once was lost but now am found, was blind, but now I see.

—John Newton (1725-1807), English Sailor,
Royal Navy, slave ship captain,
and ordained an evangelical Anglican cleric

My favorite hymn, it always moves me to tears. And when you know the writer is a former slave ship captain, it speaks to the power of redemption and gives hope to all. My husband's friend, Sonny Winston, played it on his saxophone at our wedding in Detroit, August, 1985, while my friend, Pam Higgins, read the words.

The surest way to happiness is to lose yourself in a cause greater than yourself.

—Unknown

For five years I lived this quote. I served as the Director of Development and Marketing for the National Board for Professional Teaching Standards (NBPTS). I went from an ad agency account executive to working for a cause greater than myself: certification of excellence in teaching and identifying what teachers "should know and be able to do."

My grandmother, a kindergarten and first grade teacher, and my aunt, a 9th grade English teacher, were my first teachers. I felt this was one way to honor their service, contribute to improving education, and start a new phase of my career. Turns out I was right on all counts.

This position gave me my first experience as a public speaker and as a development executive leading fundraising efforts. I also had the opportunity to participate in policy discussions with some of the smartest and most dedicated teachers, educational leaders, corporate executives and state governors: Governors Jim Hunt (D-NC), Terry Branstad (R-IA), and Tom Kean (R-NJ), Al Shanker, President of the American Federation of Teachers, Mary Hatwood Futrell, President of the National Education Association and Dr. Jim Comer (Yale). The board of directors included State Teachers of the Year from all over the United States, all were impressive, none were paid commiserate with their contributions to education. I will never forget the respect and kindness they all showed me. More respect than I have ever received in corporate America, particularly in the advertising and public relations industry. The U.S. Army (soldiers), the Catholic Church (priests) and the National Board for Professional Teaching Standards (teachers), all accepted that I had been hired because I had the knowledge and expertise to advise them on strategy and tactics in communications and marketing.

Without philosophy man cannot know what he makes; without religion he cannot know why.

—Eric Gill (1882—1940),
sculptor, typographic designer, and writer

The ability to engage in critical thinking was the most valuable skill I gained from a college education. Philosophy, ethics, religion, debate and logic courses proved to be essential in my career and essential to my continued pursuit of knowledge. In other words, yes, math and science and my marketing courses allowed me to earn a living, but the ability to think critically is a gift for a lifetime.

Battle Hymn of the Republic

Mine eyes have seen the glory of the coming of the Lord,
He is trampling out the vintage where the grapes of wrath
are stored,
He hath loosed the fateful lightning of His terrible swift sword,
His truth is marching on. *Glory! Glory! Hallelujah! His truth is
marching on.*
In the beauty of the lilies Christ was born across the sea,
with a glory in his bosom that transfigures you and me,
As He died to make men holy, let us die to make men free;
while God is marching on!

—Julia Ward Howe (1819—1910),
author and lecturer

This hymn was an inspirational song for the North and the Union soldiers, during the Civil War between the states. As a descendant of slaves and a student of history, I have an abiding interest in the Civil War period. My interest in the Civil War period was born during my time with the N.W. Ayer advertising agency in Detroit, MI. The senior vice president, Dick Prince, my supervisor, asked me to read a script for a potential PBS series General Motors planned to underwrite, The Civil War, by Ken Burns. I read it and learned so much. It was to be my project, but I received a job offer that I could not turn down and left the agency to take a job as Director of Development and Marketing for the National Board for Professional Teaching Standards (NBPTS).

During the five years, 2011-2015, of the 150th commemoration of the Civil War, my husband, Iran and I attended a number of ceremonies (Gettysburg in 2012, Burning of Columbia, 2015) and been moved emotionally by those events. One of the most moving moments, we witnessed was at one of the Sesquicentennial events commemorating the beginning of the war, April 12, 1861, occurred in Charleston, SC., at Battery Park, White Point Garden, April 12, 2011. The 1ˢᵗ Carolina (Confederate) and the 54ᵗʰ Massachusetts Colored Troops (Union) marched down the aisle, two by two, alternating, Blue and Gray, lined up in the front, facing the audience, and then the Charleston Symphony played *"Dixie"* and "The *Battle Hymn of the Republic."* How far we have come, thanks to all those brave souls who fought and died...the blessings of God to all.

Oprah Winfrey, on her business strategy: "all of my decisions in my personal life and in my public life and in my business life are based upon what is going to have meaning...so if it doesn't work with my personal internal compass, then it ain't gonna work for my business."

—Oprah Winfrey (b. 1954),
billionaire television personality and actress,
and received the Presidential Medal of Freedom, 2013

A reminder that we must have a passion for life and for the work we do. The best advice we can give to those young people, trying to figure out what career they want to pursue, is to go where their talents and interests lie. Too often, we can be consumed with how much money any particular job will pay, but I firmly believe that if you are committed to excellence then the money will come. See *Chapter 8, My Career Journey: the Only Woman in the Room.*

The happiest people don't necessarily have the best of everything, they just make the best of everything that comes along their way.

—Unknown

Growing up in rural Alabama, I had no clue that we were poor, because we had more than many in the community. Yet when I think back to the 1950's on my grandparents' farm, with no indoor plumbing, an outhouse, and no phone (party lines came in around 1955). I now recognize what we didn't have. What we had, was love, family, friends and as much food as we could eat.

If you concentrate on finding whatever is good in every situation, you will discover that your life will suddenly be filled with gratitude, a feeling that nurtures the soul.

—Rabbi Harold Kushner (b. 1935),
author, *When Bad Things Happen to Good People*

I truly believe that people are basically good, unless their actions prove differently. See Chapter 9, *Gratitude*.

Over every mountain there is a path, although it may
not be seen from the valley.

—Theodore Roethke (1908—1963),
American poet and professor (1947—1963),
and awarded the Pulitzer Prize for Poetry, 1957

We can ask God to "move that mountain." And that is exactly what I
did when I was desperately trying to figure out if my first marriage
could be saved. I went to a psychiatrist for advice and counsel and
he told me, "You must make a decision and when you do, you'll be
fine." He saved my life.

He has the right to criticize who has the heart to help.

—Abraham Lincoln (1809—1865),
16th President of U.S., 1861—1965,
and signed the Emancipation Proclamation,
January 1, 1863

Our greatest president, in my opinion, is Abraham Lincoln. An example of God's grace working through another human being, Lincoln became the great emancipator for my ancestors. Just imagine 246 years of slavery, from 1619—1865. The 13th Amendment was ratified on December 6, 1865. America was literally built on the backs of slaves, on land confiscated from the Native Americans. I must add, that of course, I respect the hard work and sacrifice of all immigrants, pioneers and patriots to the development of America.

I encourage everyone to read at least one book about Lincoln and the Civil War. My favorite book is *April 1865: The Month That Saved America,* by Jay Winik.

If we call the names of our ancestors daily, they can live forever.

—African Proverb

What a comforting thought. I attended a Kwanzaa celebration at a friend's house when we lived in Louisville, KY. It was the first day of Kwanzaa: Umoja, means unity and stresses the importance of togetherness. All the attendees were invited to say the name of an ancestor. We went around the room, one of the most inspiring moments I've ever had at a "house party."

I am the dream and the hope of the slave.
I rise
I rise
I rise.

—Maya Angelou (1928—2014),
poet, memoirist, actress,
and awarded the Presidential Medal of Freedom, 2011,
Still I Rise poem

Chapter 5.

COMMITMENT AND SUCCESS

We are what we repeatedly do.
Excellence then, is not an act, but a habit.

—Aristotle (384—322 BCE),
ancient Greek philosopher and scientist.

To laugh often and much, to win the respect of intelligent people and affection of children.

To appreciate beauty, to find the best in others.

To leave the world a little bit better, whether by a healthy child, a garden patch or a redeemed social condition.

To know even one life has breathed easier because you have lived.
This is to have succeeded.

—Ralph Waldo Emerson (1803—1882),
lecturer, poet, essayist,
and a leader in Transcendentalism, a religious, and
ethical movement
that stressed belief in the spiritual potential of every man

A certain amount of opposition is a great help to a person.
Kites rise against, not with the wind.

—John Neal (1793—1870), writer

My mother instilled in us the belief that you must work for whatever you get in this life, there are no shortcuts. Indeed there are only a small number of geniuses, the rest of us must apply ourselves in order to nurture our talents and achieve success.

Success is to be measured not so much by the position that one has reached in life as by the obstacles which he has overcome.

—Booker T. Washington,
born a slave in 1856, died in 1915,
educator and reformer,
and first president of Tuskegee University

At age sixteen, I became pregnant and my father (among others) told me I had ruined my life and would never be anything! Thank God, my mother never gave up on me; while she supported me and my son until I could figure out a way to do it myself. Eventually, I forgave my father—after he died. I now accept that he had mental problems from a head injury he received while serving in World War II.

Forgiveness allows us to move on.

There is not the slightest indication that nuclear energy will ever be obtainable. It would mean that the atom would have to be shattered at will.

—Albert Einstein (1879—1955),
German-American physicist,
won the Nobel Prize for Physics in 1921

Even the world's greatest physicist could not foresee the future and yet the future was built upon the knowledge he discovered. Let that serve as a lesson to us all to keep pursuing your passion, you never know where it will lead you.

Before you build a better mousetrap it helps to know
if there are any mice out there.

—Mortimer B. Zuckerman (b.1937),
investor, billionaire owner,
publisher of the New York Daily News,
and the U.S. News & World Report

Marketing and communications advice: do your research. Data
and research are the cornerstone of great ad campaigns, marketing
strategies, public relations and ultimately business success. Don't
assume you know the behaviors or habits of any given audience
or target group. The U.S. presidential election of 2016 has proven
how important reliability is to research and polling. Also, how
critical it is for the research analyst to filter out their own biases
and assumptions.

The time to repair the roof is when the sun is shining.

—John F. Kennedy (1917—1963),
35th President of the United States, 1961—1963

His assassination was a defining moment for baby boomers. Like most of us, I can tell you exactly what I was doing when the news of the event in Dallas was announced, washing diapers for my four-month old son, Michael. Our collective innocence was lost on that November day in 1963.

The only woman in the room and the only black person in the room for most of my career. I know it seems trite and easy to say, but it is true, if you do what you are passionate about, the money will follow: commitment and passion lead to success.

Columbus Dispatch, Business Today Section, July 29, 1996.

I served briefly as the only African-American vice president at Paul Werth. The owner was most gracious and gave me an opportunity to work on The Ohio State University account, a huge deal in Columbus, Ohio.

Chapter 6.

DIVERSITY, INCLUSION AND AMERICA

I tremble for my country when
I reflect that God is just,
that his justice cannot sleep forever.

—Thomas Jefferson, on slavery, (1743—1826),
3rd President of the United States (1801—1809), drafted the
Declaration of Independence of U.S.A.

Thomas Jefferson: a man of his time and place (sadly) who owned his children (literally).

Despite the fact that Jefferson was a slave holder, he was a brilliant man and a founder of this country. He did not live up to his knowledge of the world and history; so he remained a man of his times. Yet his words give me comfort when trying to address issues of diversity and inclusion.

Suggestion: visit Monticello, near Charlottesville, VA. When we visited, we gained an appreciation for the genius of Jefferson and a more complete understanding of the lives of the "master" (slaveholder) versus slaves like Sally Hemings, the slave and mother of his black children.

It is incredibly hard to relate to the horrible institution of slavery, but as Americans, we must understand that slavery, the Civil War and Reconstruction are at the heart of a lot of the division we still see in America.

Recommended reading:
- *Thomas Jefferson and Sally Hemings: an American Controversy*, by Annette Gordon-Reed
- *The Slaves War, the Civil War in the Words of Former Slaves*, by Andrew Ward
- *Blood at the Root, a Racial Cleansing in America*, by Patrick Phillips

Southern trees bear a strange fruit.
Blood on the leaves and blood at the root.

—Billie Holiday (1915—1959),
American jazz musician and singer

Song *"Strange Fruit"* biggest selling record of 1939, as sung by Billie
Holiday,
the song is based on a poem written in 1937 by Lewis Allan aka
Abel Meeropol,
a teacher and activist

Despite everything,
I believe that people are really good at heart.

—Anne Frank (1929—1945), German diarist,
whose diary of her Jewish family's two years in hiding in the
Netherlands,
during the Nazi occupation, is now a classic,
and required reading in most secondary schools

A diversity road warrior: sharing wisdom gained on the road to inclusion

Research has shown that most people have an "unconscious bias" toward people not like themselves. Umpires and referees will even call fewer fouls or violations on players who are from the same race as they are. Even though they have been trained to be objective and enforce the rules, it is still difficult to overcome societal norms and culture.

As individuals we have to work to overcome those biases, awareness is the first step. We each must seek out environments that are diverse—and become acquainted with people from different races and cultures. How many of your friends are different from you, in terms of race, education, ethnicity or nationality?

The workplace is the most diverse experience most of us have... the church is the least diverse. Something is wrong with that situation. Shouldn't Christians be leading the way? The answer for me is YES!

A truth about valuing diversity—follow the Platinum rule vs. the Golden Rule.

- The Golden Rule: *do unto others as you would have them do unto you.* *
- The Platinum Rule: *treat others the way they want to be treated.* **

*Matthew 7:12
***The Platinum Rule*, a book by Michael O'Connor and Tony Alessandra

Advice for human resource professionals, managers and executives

- You must know the truth, then you can tell it.
- Diversity recruitment and retention issues can have an impact on overall corporate reputation.
- External messages, involving diversity, must match the internal reality.
- Nothing is secret anymore.

How do you best explain the benefits of diversity? How we are more the same, than we are different; and that the difference is worth knowing, understanding and celebrating. If you cannot personally have all the experiences needed to reach out to others unlike you, then you must, of course, learn from the experiences of others.

In your own journey to gain knowledge about other cultures, I suggest that you read the *Cultural Health Assessment* pocket guide by D'Avanzo and Geissler.

> The ability to reach unity in diversity
> will be the greatest beauty and the
> greatest test of our civilization.*
>
> —Mahatma Gandhi (1869—1948),
> leader of the Indian Nationalist movement,
> and the father of his country

*My former employer, Bernard Hodes Group, used this quote on our premiums, e.g., coffee cups and bookmarks.

Thinking in the future tense.

—Dr. Jennifer James,
cultural anthropologist and futurist,
author, *Thinking in the Future Tense*

In my work as a diversity trainer and consultant, I encouraged executives and staff to study other cultures and recommended Dr. James' book as a must read. I highlighted more pages in her book than any I have ever read about diversity.

Cultural anthropologists seem to have the best understanding of other cultures and how groups behave. Life experience as a minority or as a person with "empathy" is not a substitute for acquiring a body of knowledge in the area of group behavior and cross-cultural skills. The best diversity practitioners understand that this work must be based on knowledge, data and not be accusatory or overtly emotional.

Equal opportunity and sexual harassment avoidance training is usually initiated to satisfy the law or settle a lawsuit and can perhaps keep your company out of trouble, but may not advance the goal of a more inclusive and diverse workforce. The goal for an employer should be to change acceptable behaviors (hiring, promotion, mentoring, and pay equity) in the workplace, not change hearts. Most employees and managers can quickly figure out what behaviors or actions are rewarded by management. Human resource managers, diversity directors and first line supervisors need a policy, guidelines, training, and authority. Clearly, the executive team and CEO must be the actual leaders and "enforcers" of an inclusive and diverse workplace.

Men stumble over the truth from time to time
but most pick themselves up and hurry
off as if nothing happened.

—Winston Churchill (1874—1965),
British statesman, orator, and author,
Prime Minister (1940—1945, 1951—1955),
and he "led his country from the brink of defeat to victory"

I continue to be interested in England and its influence on the world. How this tiny island became an empire is fascinating. From Sherlock Holmes to Agatha Christie's mysteries and all the British detective series, or think Downtown Abbey. I can spend an evening of reading or a night of Netflix with the fictional and the real history of the people of the United Kingdom.

Prejudice is the burden that confuses the past,
threatens the future and renders the present inaccessible.

—Maya Angelou (1928—2014),
poet, memoirist, actress,
and awarded the Presidential Medal of Freedom, 2011

What can we each do about prejudice? Do not tolerate it and speak up about injustice when we see it. An example: one of my white female friends, in Coral Springs, FL, had a party with people from all backgrounds. One of the reasons we loved South Florida is because it is a cultural melting pot. One couple started talking about "Jews" in a negative way, the hostess told them they had to leave, now! That is how we move toward a more inclusive society in our everyday social lives, by standing up for your values and for "right" even when it is uncomfortable.

The cause of freedom is not the
cause of a race or a sect,
a party or a class—it is the cause of humankind,
the very birthright of humanity.

—Anna Julia Cooper, born a slave in 1858,
died in 1964, at age 105,
and served as principal of M Street/Dunbar High School,
Washington D. C.

Quote from *First Class: The Legacy of Dunbar, America's First Black Public High School,* by journalist, Alison Stewart.

An amazing statistic about "freedom" in America is that around 9,000 black patriots served in the Revolutionary War's Continental Army and Navy, as soldiers, cooks, cobblers, servants and blacksmiths.

Black people have fought in all U.S. wars and are the most patriotic of Americans. Why do I say that? We fought even when we were not free and were living under slavery, the threat of lynching and Jim Crow segregationist laws. We are truly patriots.

Recommended reading:
- *American Patriots: The Story of Blacks in the Military from the Revolution to Desert Storm*, by Gail Lumet Buckley. Interesting to note that she is the daughter of the great singer and actress, Lena Horne.

- *Brothers in Arms: The Epic Story of the 761st Tank Battalion, WWII's Forgotten Heroes*, by Kareem Abdul-Jabbar and Anthony Walton.

Diversity training usually enumerates the dimensions of diversity, so the audience starts from the same knowledge base. The dimensions of diversity are age, race, gender, disability/ability, sexual orientation and nationality. I am often asked if religion is a dimension of diversity, the answer is no. We can change our religion, we cannot change the way we are born except in extraordinary circumstances related to gender identity.

However I still believe, we humans are more alike than we are different but we must know, understand and respect the differences.

We are not asking for a color blind society, just to be treated equally by the legal system, in hiring and promotion, in financial transactions, housing and by the majority society. Seems simple to me, but oh how difficult it can be.

Hiring and compensation are a particular barrier. Given a choice and no directive from the company, managers and first-line supervisors will hire someone who has a similar background and is most like them. If bonuses and promotions are tied to the diversity of your staff and the ability to mentor others not like yourself, it will move the needle and increase the diversity of your organization. Leadership must come from the top, preferably the chief executive officer and the executive committee.

One of challenges of implementing change within any institution is a natural resistance to changing long held assumptions about who makes a good employee or manager. If the company is NOT currently diverse, you will continue to make the same sort of hires until senior management, preferably the chief executive officer (CEO), indicates that kind of biased behavior will no longer be rewarded and shows a commitment to diversity from the board room to the mail room. Managers are quite good at responding to the CEO's imperatives.

You must learn to comfort the afflicted and afflict the comfortable.

—Finley Peter Dunne (1867—1936), humorist and writer, his essays as "***Mr. Dooley***" were read at Theodore Roosevelt's cabinet meetings

The trick to being a "truth teller" to power is to do it diplomatically, but firmly. If you are the only African American and the only woman in the room, and you are treated unjustly or see injustice, you must speak up. In fact, if you are in a leadership role, you have a duty to educate the ignorant or defend those without a place at the table. And of course, make diverse hires. The problem for black women in the workplace is to counter the stereotype of "the angry black woman," while still confronting injustice. Our experience in America has inclined many of us to a willingness to speak truth to power. In other words, not go along to get along.

The years I spent working for DuPont in advertising, for clients that included the U.S. Army Recruiting Command, General Motors and Ford, were some of the most exciting years of my career. Not coincidentally, they were all linked in business. DuPont helped in the founding of General Motors and through leadership or products did business with each other, e.g., General Motors Defense and the U.S. Defense Department. Therefore, when I interviewed with General Motors' ad agency, they were impressed that I had worked for DuPont and for the U.S. Army. General Motors Defense was glad to have a black female account executive on the team who had actually worked for and with military officers and soldiers.

From *A Tale of Two Cities*:
it was the best of times, it was the worst of times.

—Charles Dickens (1812—1870),
English novelist, one of the greatest ever

I have loved Dickens since junior high school English class. *A Christmas Carol* is one of my favorites. I highly recommend *American Notes for General Circulation,* a travelogue based on his trip to America in 1842, with unique observations on the New World. His commentary about the institution of slavery in the U.S.A. is particularly gut-wrenching. He paints a vivid picture of the violence perpetrated on families and on both male and female slaves.

Research is a loss of innocence.

—Unknown

This is one of my favorite quotes. It makes the case for how important research and analysis of the demographics of your current employee population along with projections about the makeup of the future workforce, can be on developing diversity recruitment strategies that are objective and that work. However, the real challenge is to convince senior management and first-line supervisors of the need to change hiring and promotion practices. Also, research can compel you to discard assumptions about a particular culture or stereotypes, and instead rely on objective data and facts.

As an Asian American, you're constantly confronted with race, but you don't have that prominent a role in the discussion.

—Hua Hsu (b. 1977),
Chinese-American music writer, N.Y. Times,
and an English professor at Vassar College

One of my earliest learning experiences in diversity occurred when I attended a conference for diversity and human resources professionals in Miami. The speaker complimented us all on how smart we were. Then he asked for a show of hands, how many of you are college graduates? Have Masters Degrees? Have PhDs and then asked us to "Name an Asian-American hero?" No one in the audience of about 300, could.

As soon as I got home, I called an Asian man with the Asian American Association of South Florida. I had met him a few weeks earlier. I described what happened and my embarrassment at not being able to answer the question. Around midnight, I received a six-page fax from him, with page after page of Asian-American heroes/heroines.

From that point on, I used this question to capture the attention of participants in my training sessions. Name an Asian-American hero or heroine? Typical answer is Michele Kwan, a much admired and talented Asian-American ice-skater, but not a heroine outside of sports. If you want to learn a few of the names and their heroic actions, do the research.

Hint: Japanese soldiers who served heroically in World War II, despite their families forced internment in U.S. camps.

Many a small thing has been made large by the right kind of advertising.*

—Mark Twain (1835—1910),
the pseudonym of Samuel L. Clemens,
humorist, journalist, lecturer and novelist,
he wrote *The Adventures of Huckleberry Finn* and
The Adventures of Tom Sawyer

*Given my career in advertising, I can relate to Mark Twain's assessment of the value of advertising and its ability to persuade in the hands of the right creative team. N.W. Ayer used to show prospective clients a highlight reel of all the groundbreaking, enduring print and broadcast ads and the taglines we had developed over the years. I am proud to have worked for this organization, despite diversity and inclusion problems with one or two supervisors. The Army ads could bring tears to your eyes.

A few of the notable campaigns:

AT&T: *"Reach out and touch someone."*
U.S. Army: *"Be all you can be."*
DeBeers: *"A diamond is forever."*
Morton Salt: *"When it rains it pours."*
R.J. Reynolds Tobacco: *"I'd walk a mile for a camel."*

Chapter 7.

LAUGHTER HEALS

If high heels were so wonderful,
Men would still be wearing them.

—Sue Grafton (b. 1940), mystery writer,
known for her alphabet mystery series,
and private detective, Kinsey Millhone, **A is for Alibi**, 1982

Life is a shipwreck, but we must not
forget to sing in the lifeboats.

—Voltaire (1694—1778),
French philosopher and writer,
and a crusader against tyranny, bigotry and cruelty

Music and singing heal the heart, inspire and make us feel better. The blues is the music that speaks to my soul and my life. Although I have every genre of music in my library: rock, country, folk, classical, Broadway, rap, gospel and a lot of R&B from the 60's through to today. You can tell a lot about how open-minded or sheltered a person is by the music they enjoy.

To err is human, but to really foul things up requires a computer.

—Anonymous

My employer in the 1980's, the New York ad agency, N.W. Ayer's Detroit Office, had a sign in the reception area: "to Ayer is human." I still don't get it. Were we asking for forgiveness, if we made a mistake in an ad? Perhaps it was designed to provoke thought and discussion.

A gossip is one who talks to you about others,
A bore is one who talks to you about himself, and
A brilliant conversationalist is one
who talks to you about yourself.

—Lisa Kirk (1925—1990),
American actress and singer

One of the best decisions I ever made, was to switch my major from accounting to interpersonal communications. I even had the opportunity to conduct the interpersonal labs with incoming communications majors at Cleveland State University. The ability to communicate, the spoken and written word, cannot be overstated. It proved to be the key to my success in the corporate world.

The hardest years in life are those between ten and
seventy.

—Helen Hayes (at 73) (1900—1993),
award-winning actress on stage, film and television,
awarded the Presidential Medal of Freedom, 1986

We can all relate to the difficulties we encounter moving from
childhood to maturity and can only hope that she is right about
life after seventy.

We can't all be heroes because
somebody has to sit on the curb
and clap as they go by.

—Will Rogers (1879—1935),
humorist and entertainer

Will Rogers, what a funny and wise man.

Whatever women must do they must do twice as well as men to be thought half as good. Luckily, this is not difficult.

—Charlotte Whitton (1896—1975),
Canadian feminist and former mayor of Ottawa

Just kidding. When you are the only woman in the room, you better be prepared in your area of expertise. And most importantly, have at least one ally or mentor among the men in the room or around the table. Fortunately, there are usually other women in the room now, but typically only one woman of color.

I have yet to hear a man ask for advice on how to combine marriage and a career.

—Gloria Steinem (b. 1934),
feminist, political activist and editor of *Ms. Magazine*

I am a feminist. Although as a black woman, that identity is somewhat complicated. Given cultural norms in our American society, I must be African American first, then female. Each identity has its own set of joys and consequences. At one time, we were called a "two-fer," you get a woman and a person of color when a black female is hired (cynical, I know, but true). The stats on wages and income, tell us that Black women are at the bottom of the pyramid with the lowest wages of all demographic groups, Caucasian men and women, have been at the top f-o-r-e-v-e-r, now Hispanics and Asians are beginning to change that dynamic in the workplace.

Just when you think you've graduated from the school of experience someone thinks up a new course.

—Mary H. Waldrip (b.1949),
writer and English nurse

Humor helps us keep our perspective and moves us forward on our journey.

Humor is laughing at what you haven't
got, when you ought to have it.

—Langston Hughes (1902—1967),
American poet, novelist, playwright,
and columnist

As a teenager, I was an avid reader of Langston Hughes. I loved his
"Simple" short stories.

Chapter 8.

MY CAREER JOURNEY THE ONLY WOMAN IN THE ROOM

And often the only black person too.

I wouldn't take nothing for my journey now
Come too far to turn around.

—Chorus, Old-Time Gospel Hymn

I have had a glorious career in public relations, advertising and diversity consulting. But I owe it to my daughters and sisters-in-the-spirit to address the incredible stress African-American women can be under when they feel they are representing their race and their gender, as the only one in the room. They want to pave the way for others and at the same time deliver excellence in the same way white executives are allowed to work. Not have to work twice as hard for less recognition and less pay. To quote my step-daughter, Tahlia: "I sometimes feel that black women in the workplace are only allowed two emotions: happy or angry." We have to keep smiling or something is wrong and are sometimes expected to speak for all people of African descent.

I-m-p-o-s-s-i-b-l-e!

My hope is that one or more of the quotes, poems or songs in this book will make the burden that is particular to women, and specific to black women, easier to bear and the journey smoother and more joyous.

For most of my career, I have indeed been the only woman in the room and often the only *person of color* in the room. I have also had the joy and great good luck of being in the right place at the right time performing jobs that I loved.

1970's and 1980's—College Pays Off
Wilmington, Delaware

The DuPont Company paid for my college education and after graduation hired me in the Public Relations Department at corporate headquarters in Wilmington, DE. I am forever grateful for the training and experiences I had with DuPont and the pension for my years of service.

They made sure every new employee had a mentor and received all the training needed to do your job at the level of excellence expected of all employees. Delaware is a beautiful state and it was a pleasure to work there. Living on the East Coast was quite a bit more expensive than I anticipated and proved very difficult for me to manage as a single mother. Thank God I was blessed to meet good friends who were there for me when I needed help, including financial.

Detroit, Michigan: Motown. I found my love there.

My daughter, Angela, and I will never forget our first trip to Detroit together. I accepted a position as a technical sales representative with Parker Chemicals, a division of Occidental Petroleum. We went to Northland Center, a mall in Southfield (closed in 2015), and just sat down and looked at all the black people in one place and could not stop smiling. Though we loved Delaware and our home, we were definitely in the minority in our community.

I was the first woman, first black person and first non-engineer to join the sales team for Parker Chemicals. I was hired thanks to my mentor and former supervisor (at the DuPont Plant in Cleveland), Steve Gerow, who had left DuPont to become Director of Sales and was my advocate. I had to learn metallurgy and the processes for cleaning and plating metals. But given that I am a life-long student, I enjoyed the learning, but ultimately, not "technical sales" nor the "male locker room" environment. I was expected to take my clients to "lingerie" lunches, where women modeled lingerie— think Victoria's Secret—at the local suburban restaurant.

Get mad, then get over it.
Perpetual optimism is a force multiplier.

—Colin Powell (b. 1937), a U.S. Army General,
first African American chairman of the Joint Chiefs,
and first African American Secretary of State

1980's—My "Mad Men" Years in Advertising and Public Relations

My years of experience working for the Department of Defense, Armed Forces Examining and Entrance Station, allowed me to move on to a new position. I went to work for my old DuPont ad agency, N.W. Ayer & Son, America's first and oldest advertising agency, founded in Philadelphia, PA in 1869. Ayer had the longest running relationship with a client, AT&T, for seventy-five years. They had created memorable ad campaigns with taglines that made marketing history for companies, such as, DeBeers (*A Diamond is Forever*) and the U.S. Army (*Be All You Can Be*).

While at N.W. Ayer, I worked as the Regional Account Executive on the U.S. Army Recruiting Command account, for the State of Michigan, for three years. I also worked on the General Motors Corporate Public Relations account for two years.

U.S. Army Recruiting Command: *"Be All You Can Be"*

DuPont was a client of N.W. Ayer, my account executive recommended me for a position on the U.S. Army account. I was hired by the New York office, in 1982, as the first African-American female regional account representative, to work on the U.S. Army account, for the State of Michigan. I had the opportunity to travel all over Michigan in support of the advertising campaign, media buying and public relations efforts for U.S. Army Recruiting Command at Fort Sheridan, Illinois. My regional manager was based in our Chicago offices on Wacker Drive. When I first started on the Army account, the enlisted men would stop by to have casual chats with me—my office was across from the executive officer's. He finally told the military folks that I should be treated the same way they would treat a "major" in uniform. From that point on, I participated in all senior level staff meetings, including briefings for senior staff and visiting generals. I briefed them on the status of current marketing, advertising and public relations plans in support of the Army's recruiting campaign. I loved working with this client with such a dedicated staff who respected our expertise. If you held a certain rank (remember, I was a "major") then you were expected to have a certain level of knowledge and be treated accordingly, no matter what your race or gender. I also enjoyed watching change of command ceremonies and attending the military balls. Whenever a military band performs in the Columbia, South Carolina, Fort Jackson area, we go to see them, particularly the Old Guard.

During my time working on the U.S. Army account for N.W. Ayer New York, I had three offices. One office was in the Fisher Building, a gorgeous art deco building with the most magnificent elevator doors, with N.W. Ayer Detroit. Another office was in the Army's Detroit Battalion in Greek town, and the third office was in Lansing, Michigan. Basically I lived in my car. I attended four Christmas parties in New York City, Chicago, Detroit and the Army annual Christmas ball for the Detroit Battalion.

After three years, the Detroit office hired me to work on the General Motors account. The Detroit office primarily handled General Motors corporate public relations and advertising. I was the only African-American account executive, the only other black person in the office was the receptionist. I lived AMC's *"Mad Men"* television series about the glory years of advertising agencies, including the three martini lunches. The general manager had a bar in his office for entertaining clients. At 5:00 p.m., the account and creative team would gather in his office with a few of our clients and have wine and cocktails. I was one of two females invited. That's where I learned to make vodka gimlets.

The Fisher Building, built in 1928, in the New Center area, was across the street from GM Headquarters, with a tunnel connecting the two buildings. I had occasion to attend meetings on the 14th floor where the General Motors executive offices were located. At that time, there were no senior female executives or African Americans on the 14th floor. Roger Smith was CEO. Toward the end of my employment with N.W. Ayer, GM hired one African-American senior executive, Roy Roberts, to lead Human Resources.

Roberts was quoted in Forbes Magazine: "I've been the first black everywhere I went. One of my jobs is to make sure I am not the last." Now, General Motors has Mary Barra, promoted in 2014 as the first female CEO of a car company. What an amazing and well-deserved advance for women in the car business.

I considered myself lucky and fortunate to have worked in the automotive industry, which has served as a "vehicle" for middle class mobility. I am so glad, President Obama supported a bail out for General Motors and not just because my husband kept his job. The automotive industry accepted Affirmative Action and has maintained a commitment to diversity and equal opportunity for many years.

My interest in the Civil War was stirred when General Motors sponsored the first Ken Burns, PBS documentary, *The Civil War*. I was one of the first people to read the entire script and give my enthusiastic support for the sponsorship, and the rest is history.

I also handled a couple of *pro bono* accounts: the Detroit Symphony and the Sacred Heart Seminary recruitment campaign. The Sacred Heart Seminary pitch was held at the Archdiocese of Detroit offices and included the archbishop. The more unusual part of our preparations for the meeting was the briefing the account team received from our Catholic creative director. He briefed the art director (Jewish) and me (United Church of Christ) on proper Catholic etiquette. We did *not* have to kiss his ring.

After we won the business, I gathered all the research for the team on the Catholic Church and status of the priesthood, including the demographics and behavior of our target audience. The average age of a priest was sixty-five and was majority white non-Hispanic. The objective of the creative strategy was to reach young men, particularly minority and Spanish speakers. Our tagline: *"We Want to Collar a Few Good Men."* We received lots of mail from nuns objecting to that tagline. Some of the Catholic orders for nuns have decided to let their orders die out and certainly do not do the kind of outreach Scared Heart Seminary was now engaged in doing for the first time. We developed radio and television advertising and outdoor billboards. The campaign advertised on Rock, Top 40 Pop, R&B and Country radio stations. We also ran an ad in Sports Illustrated's regional edition and a local television ad during Saturday Night Live. Inquiries poured in. Father West assured us that only those who are "called by God" are ultimately accepted into the seminary.

This campaign was featured on ABC National News and received world-wide attention. This was the first time television, radio, print and outdoor was used to reach young men, between ages eighteen and twenty-five, and invite them to become priests. Results: the Detroit archbishop was promoted to the Vatican in Rome; and I was able to get my Catholic mother-in-law a ticket to the mass given in Detroit, by the visiting Pope John Paul II.

A famous conservative columnist
and a client luncheon

A noted conservative columnist (still active) was the invited speaker for a private lunch with our General Motors client. Of course, as during much of my career in public relations and advertising, I was "the only black woman in the room." This was during the early 80's, when Nelson Mandela was still in prison and the world had imposed economic sanctions on South Africa and its apartheid policies. The speaker was fascinating, but just as he was making his conservative pitch for a different approach to handling South Africa, I had to go the bathroom. I was sure if I got up, my client and the agency's general manager would assume that I was conducting my own personal protest. Based on my values, I had recently turned down a promotion to work on the South African based DeBeers Diamonds account and relocation to New York City. *I went to the bathroom.*

DeBeers client meetings were held in Switzerland, not in the U.S.A., because it was a considered a cartel which is illegal in the U.S.A. Account service included global travel, as well as lots of travel to international trade shows, meetings with jewelers and fashion editors, and a huge ad budget to produce television ads for the campaign, *"Diamonds are forever."*

I am still proud of the fact that I had the fortitude to turn down the *glamour* account in advertising at the time and a job in New York City...the place of my dreams. My consolation prize was promotion to senior account executive on the General Motors Defense account with the tagline, *"GM: The Ultimate Ally."*

1990's—Public Relations and the Call to Serve

Detroit, Michigan: fundraising for a noble purpose

I left N.W. Ayer, in 1988, to move into another career, as a development and public relations executive at this new non-profit, the National Board for Professional Teaching Standards (NBPTS), whose mission was to "certify excellence in teaching and determine what a teacher should know and be able to do." I was one of the first four people hired by the CEO, Jim Kelly, and eventually became the corporate secretary to the board of directors. I had the privilege of working with corporate leaders in education reform, Governors Jim Hunt of North Carolina, Tom Kean of New Jersey and Terry Branstad, Iowa, as well as excellent teachers from around the United States; and with union leaders, Mary Futrell, President of the National Education Association (NEA), and Al Shanker, President of the American Federation of Teachers (AFT).

Teaching is not a lost art,
but the regard for it is a lost tradition.*

—Jacques Barzun (1907 – 2012)
Professor, historian and author
Columbia University

*This quote was featured in a brochure about the National Board for Professional Teaching Standards. Thanks to our collaboration with our PR firm, Widmeyer & Associates, based in Washington, DC, we won a number of creative awards for our marketing and communications work, including the prestigious Silver Anvil, from the Public Relations Society of America. Scott Widmeyer was a mentor and friend. He recommended me for a position in the Clinton White House. I didn't get an interview, but still treasure the referral.

How I met Lee Iacocca, former Chief Executive Officer of Chrysler

Iacocca wrote an editorial, in The Detroit News, about the need to improve public education in America. The NBPTS CEO, Jim Kelly and I wrote a letter to him about our mission. He read it, his staff contacted us and we met with his public relations team, all of which resulted in a gift of $250,000 directly from him in San Diego. During my time at the National Board for Professional Teaching Standards, we raised over $6,000,000.

When you work for a non-profit with an important mission, you work long hours and hopefully with passion. I realized after a few years, that while we were making progress toward certification of excellence, the transformation of the public school system was going to take many, many years.

Public Relations and Advertising Industry

I gave education reform and the National Board my all. After we had a major downsizing of employees and some good people that I had hired were let go, I started looking to get back into the for-profit world of public relations and advertising. Just by happenstance, I was seated next to the wife of the CEO of Campbell and Company, a public relations firm, at a Detroit Club luncheon. We started talking, and the next thing I knew, I became their first African-American vice president. I had a staff of six and handled public relations for all events for Ford Motor Company's marketing and public relations functions, including NASCAR, the Detroit Gran Prix, PGA Golf at the TPC, and auto shows. We also supported the Ford North American Operations head, Bob Rewey, in his work as the chairman of the Detroit Police Athletic League. This job was the most fun you could have and still get paid while doing it.

White men and women are the rule, people of color are the exception, in public relations and advertising. Not only was I the only black woman in the room for most in-house and client meetings, I was also one of a few that were members of the local chapters of the Advertising Club and the Public Relations Society of America...in Detroit, Louisville, Columbus, Miami and Columbia, SC. And that still holds true today. While both industries, particularly advertising, have been called to account, by officials of New York City, for their lack of diversity, they continue to lag behind the demographic makeup of the population of the U.S.A. The lack of diversity continues even though their client contacts are increasingly diverse. Whenever I had the power to hire, I hired the best person for the job and "for diversity."

Louisville, Kentucky: the Kentucky Derby and Muhammad Ali's Hometown

We left Detroit and moved to Louisville, KY because my husband was transferred by General Motors, Buick Division. As a newspaper junkie, my next job was a dream job, marketing manager with the Courier Journal, a Gannett newspaper company. The people in Louisville are the nicest and most welcoming of any city we have lived in to date.

We attended the Kentucky Derby and Festival, thoroughbred horse racing, which lasts for two weeks, and The Oaks, the day before the Derby. The Oaks is used as fundraiser for charities. We had the opportunity to sit in Millionaires Row, a once in a lifetime occasion. You cannot live in Kentucky and not get caught up in thoroughbred horse racing and college basketball. Kentucky or Louisville: you must make a choice, we chose Louisville.

One of my most memorable assignments was to represent the newspaper on a committee to establish a museum in honor of boxer and hometown hero, Muhammad Ali. We had extensive photo archives of his years in Louisville and of his boxing career. I participated in discussions with members of Muhammad Ali's family and others to lay the ground work for the establishment of a Muhammad Ali museum. That particular effort failed. A museum was later established called the Muhammad Ali Center and dedicated to educational programming for young adults. Muhammad Ali died on June 3rd, 2016. I am so glad that we had an opportunity to meet him and that his hometown honored him. A town that had rejected him came to embrace him.

> He who is not courageous enough to take
> risks will accomplish nothing in life.
>
> —Muhammad Ali (1942—2016),
> boxer and activist,
> and the "GOAT" (Greatest of All Time)

I am proud to have played a small role in furthering the mission of this interactive, international center: "to preserve and share the legacy and ideals of Muhammad Ali, to promote respect, hope, and understanding, and to inspire adults and children everywhere to be as great as they can be." His memorial service reflected his vision of a diverse and inclusive society: participants included Buddhists, Muslims, Christians, Black, White and Native Americans.

Columbus, Ohio: The Ohio State University, Go Bucks!

Once again, I followed my husband to his next assignment for General Motors in Columbus, OH. I was hired, as a vice president, at a well-known and respected public relations agency, Paul Werth & Associates. Once again, I was the only African-American female executive. My clients included The Ohio State University Fisher School of Business and the Athletic Department. The owner of the firm hired me as a "change agent," and I was welcomed by all. However, my management style did not mesh well within the environment as it existed. Also, I did not have enough allies to be that change agent. Still, it was a good experience and taught me to "look before I leap" when making a job decision. I met a number of movers and shakers in the community and built a network that allowed me to move on to a position as the Marketing and Public Relations Manager with the Wexner Center for the Arts at The Ohio State University. The Wexner Center was named after Lex Wexner, multi-millionaire retailer and major donor to the university. Since the Wexner Center was a contemporary art museum (film, dance and the visual arts), one of the interview questions was: what is art? I guess my answer passed muster.

My experiences in Columbus were memorable. I gained valuable insight and knowledge about public relations from the agency side and about entertainment marketing at the Wexner Center for the Arts. While I like the Expressionists, I did acquire an understanding and even appreciation for contemporary works of art.

2000's—Back in the Ad Business

Fort Lauderdale, Coral Springs FL and Columbia, SC: working from home is a blessing

I became a tele-commuter while working as the Vice President and National Director of Diversity Services reporting to our New York City office. I had the opportunity to work in recruitment advertising and diversity during my twelve years at Bernard Hodes Group, a division of Omnicom Group, a global advertising company. Many of my clients were Fortune 1,000 companies, from Heineken to Ryder Systems to Corning. I did workshops at human resources conferences and with government agencies, such as, the IRS, National Park Service and others.

Love South Beach, A1A and Las Olas Blvd.

South Florida residents feel like they're on vacation all the time, even when you work.

The rich, the poor, and celebrities seem to all be on equal footing, just enjoying the laid back style of South Florida. My clients included: Royal Caribbean, Ryder Systems, Tyco and Office Depot. We had more visitors and house guests during this time than ever before. All of our guests wanted to go to South Beach in Miami to sight see and perhaps spot a few celebrities out partying. The only celebrity I met, was LaTanya Richardson, actress and wife of Samuel L. Jackson, when she filled in for him at a Design Center event in Fort Lauderdale. I was so impressed with how humble and down-to-earth she was; and I continue to root for her and her acting career.

Our home was on a lake in Coral Springs, we eventually bought a second home on Hutchinson Island, near Fort Pierce. It was a condo that we rented out to the snowbirds during the winter months. I spent the summers (HOT) up there during the week and Iran came up on the weekends. We spent four years in Coral Springs, leaving in 2002, when General Motors transferred Iran to Columbia, SC. We could have stayed in South Florida forever.

September 11, 2001: changed business travel forever...

My keynote speaking engagements started in Fort Lauderdale and grew over the years. The joy of traveling for business was taken away by terrorists on that beautiful September morning. No matter how many reward points accumulated for free hotel nights or air travel, the stress counter balanced the traveling experience. Delays, long lines, travel alerts, no more valet parking (I know, boo hoo) all are now a permanent part of traveling by air. Hodes did allow limo pickup from home and airports, a wonderful perk, after 9/11. I traveled about 60% of the time, and worked from a home office. The ability to work from home is perfect for advertising, public relations and sales people. You don't have to attend meetings in person, no office chit chat and you can concentrate on work. The new mobile technology has allowed many people, particularly women, to manage a career and maintain a good balance with family life.

Diversity in recruitment and hiring matter. Inclusion matters for retention.

Based on my diverse experiences and ad background, I worked with Bernard Hodes Group, a recruitment ad agency, as a diversity trainer, consultant and speaker. From the time I started with Hodes in 1998, I traveled all over the United States to counsel clients on strategies for recruiting and hiring a diverse employee population. I also learned how to be an effective trainer with not-so-diverse staffs, including a number of executive committees. I truly appreciate my time with Hodes for the experiences and opportunities.

Nothing is permanent, accept change
The economy suffered severely in 2008 and diversity and recruitment advertising consultants were expendable within corporate human resources budgets. In 2010, my department was eliminated and my staff and I were downsized out of the company. If you have never been called on the phone and told your job and you are no longer needed, I can tell you, it hurts. For the first time in my life, I collected unemployment.

Later, I started my own consulting business, Cummings & Company, LLC. That's when I started thinking about writing this book to encourage others to *be fearless* while pursuing their dreams.

We have been privileged to have second homes in beautiful locations—Hutchinson Island, FL (Jensen Beach, right on the Atlantic Ocean), Hendersonville, NC (Laurel Park, the town on the mountain), and Shaker Heights, OH (back home in the Cleveland area, after over 20 years away). Our second homes provided a getaway, retreat and vacation place. We were so blessed to spend time on the shores of the Atlantic Ocean and the mountains of North Carolina. Our last second home in Shaker Hts. was a chance to go home again...and yes you can go home again and reconnect with friends from high school and even elementary school.

Fortunately, my telecommuting job and all the wonderful tech tools, allowed me to work in two locations, as long as I could get to an airport. Imagine, two black children, who both lived for a time in Garden Valley, one of Cleveland's low-income housing projects, had enough success to own two homes, one a vacation home. We have wonderful memories, of places and people. We will always cherish that phase of our lives.

We currently reside in Columbia, South Carolina, one home is fine with us. We love our house and friends, yet continue to adjust to the segregated nature of the culture of South Carolina. We plan to stay here, now that the Confederate flag is off the State Capital grounds.

South Carolina State Motto
Latin: "Dum Spiro Spero"
"While I Breathe, I Hope."

That's me, receiving a $250,000 check from Lee Iacocca, former CEO of Chrysler Corporation, for the National Board for Professional Teaching Standards.

Love cars and the people who make them.

The journey of a thousand miles
begins with a single step.

—Lao-tzu (604BC—531BC)
The Way of Lao-tzu,
Chinese Philosopher

Plenty to do, some retire, while others carry on.

—Bill Cunningham (1929—2016)
Photographer,
NYT Sunday Style

You must decide what you want to do and then do it...harder than it sounds. I have always lived by "to do lists," and long-term goals, which help you figure out next steps and keep you on track and moving forward.

A Few Pictures from My Journey

It is in the shelter of each other, that the people live.

—Irish Proverb

Carol, Iran, me, and Tahlia at my surprise 60th birthday party in Fort Lauderdale. Carol, my manager, instigated this event with Iran and Tahlia, my stepdaughter. I still smile when I remember Tahlia, with her beautiful voice, singing *My Favorite Things*, revised and personalized just for me, ending in "Bloody Mary."

Angela and Tim's wedding,
Michael, Angie, and Me.
December, 2014

My brothers, LaDon (deceased) and William
With our mother, Virgie.
Our former home in Shaker Heights, OH.

Gettysburg National Park Visitor Center

Chapter 9.

GRATITUDE

Call someone from your past and tell them thanks.

—Brad Meltzer (b.1970),
novelist, political thrillers

My thanks and gratitude to all those who influenced, encouraged and helped me attain my career goals. I am blessed beyond measure. And for making my career and life trip a joy, filled with laughter, adventure and love, thanks to my husband, Iran S. Cummings. To my mother, brothers, children, grandchildren, and great grandchildren, thanks for your understanding, patience and love.

One of my great pleasures is to watch readings by authors during book festivals on C-Span Book TV. I heard the mystery writer, Brad Meltzer, talk about his book, *The Fifth Assassin*. His personal philosophy, he described as having an "attitude of gratitude" and suggested that we should all: "call someone from your past and tell them you are thankful" for the help they gave you in your life.

In that spirit, I compiled my grateful list in order of their appearance in my career and life: Mr. Blackwell, Pat and Jerry Parker, Connie Jones, Tom Wood, Steve Gerow, Valerie Cross, Bob Taylor, Joyce Bembry, Eileen Shea, Brent McCutheon, Lt. Col. Kool, Mary Harper, Jackie Vaughn, Bob Kingsbury, Dick Prince, Bruce Engelson, Toni DeClercq, Doug Marshall, Cecile Keith-Brown, James A. Kelly, former Governor Jim Hunt (NC), Scott Widmeyer, Rebecca Schrader, Rod Campbell, Mrs. Campbell, Carrie Poletti, Dick Tobin, Helen Love, Linda Pursell, Wayne Brown, Sandy Harbrecht, Carol Williams, Patrick McCusker, Jenny Zimmer, Ann Bremner, Les Wright, Donna James, Karen Swarzwalder, Elise Wright Barnes, Carol Barber, Annette Browdy, Sean Broderick, Dedra Paul, Martha Ceja, Sam Hines, Paul Seal, Gerri Rocker, Opal Comfort, Nancy Rehbine, Ernest McFadden, Frank Scruggs, Alexandra Bassil, Michael Wheeler, Lisa Gaynier, Pat Rose, Shaunice Hawkins, Vickie McClary, Joyce Jenkins, Rev. Danny Murphy, and Steve Sawyer.

The quotes in this book represent words that have inspired me. I hope my journey and the quotes will provide inspiration to others.

I asked some of the people listed above to share quotes that helped them overcome challenges or served as a guidepost throughout their lives. They graciously provided their insights and inspirational words.

Cecile Keith-Brown, founder and principal of the philanthropic services firm, Meaningful Giving, has more than twenty years of experience working with donors, volunteer leaders and grant making institutions as a non-profit executive. She is a highly accomplished, knowledgeable philanthropy professional with extensive experience working with individuals and family foundations. She has in-depth knowledge of charitable giving strategies, planned giving vehicles, and estate planning. She has held executive leadership positions with the University of Michigan, Chicago Children's Museum, the Museum of Science and Industry, and Wayne State University. Cecile is also an assistant physical therapist, clinical massage therapist and Reiki Master. She has a practice in the Chicago area.

"No anger, no worry, no fear." A variation of the Reiki mantra that is no worry, no anger. This is a key concept of Reiki (a form of energy healing). Cecile added 'no fear' since fear has been a key obstacle to her peace of mind.

"Can I help you?" One of the things that Cecile's mother (Dr. Rachel Boone Keith) taught her...to always ask others. This has shaped her spirit of immediately helping. That's why she'll walk into a kitchen at a party and start working by clearing dishes, even if it's not her event or her kitchen.

Relationship: client and friend

Impact on my life:
Cecile was my Detroit Symphony client contact and became one of my best friends. She referred me to the National Board for Professional Teaching Standards position. That position enhanced and changed my career. I am forever grateful to Cecile, one of the most gracious people I know.

James A. Kelly has had a distinguished career in education policy, education finance, philanthropy, and teaching standards, assessments and certification. He is Senior Advisor to the President of the National Board for Professional Teaching Standards, and chairs the Board of Advisors for Teaching Works, a new teacher education initiative at the University of Michigan. From 1987—1999, Mr. Kelly was founding President and CEO of the National Board for Professional Teaching Standards (NBPTS), where he led efforts to create National Board Certification (NBC), the US's advanced professional certification program for accomplished elementary and secondary teachers. Almost all states provide recognition for NBC and over 100,000 teachers have become National Board Certified. Mr. Kelly is co-chair of Learning to Give, a non-profit project that has worked with teachers to develop over 1,500 on-line teaching units to help students learn about volunteerism. He is a trustee of the Cranbrook Educational Community, in Bloomfield Hills, Michigan, has chaired its Art Museum Committee, and is vice-chair of the Governing Board of the Cranbrook Art Academy. Mr. Kelly has four children and seven grandchildren. His wife, Mariam C. Noland, is president of the Community Foundation for Southeast Michigan.

PHILOSOPHY OF LIFE

A Master in the Art of Living draws no sharp distinction between his work and his play, his labor and his leisure, his mind and his body, his education and his recreation. He hardly knows which is which. He simply pursues his vision of excellence through whatever he is doing, and leaves to others to determine whether he is working or playing. To himself, he always appears to be doing both.

—Francoise-Auguste-Rene, vicomte de Chateaubriand
(1768–1848),
French author and diplomat

Relationship: former President of the National Board for Professional Teaching Standards

<u>Impact on my life:</u>
Jim gave me an opportunity to work to change education in America and develop as an executive. As corporate secretary, I had the opportunity to work with the Board of Directors and learn how to implement plans within a large diverse environment. My opinions were valued by leaders in U.S. education policy and treated with respect. Finally, this was the beginning of my career as a public speaker and trainer.

Carol Barber has more than thirty years of experience in talent acquisition, recruitment advertising and employment branding. She spent the majority of her career with Bernard Hodes Group (BHG), where she supported national employers across all industries and managed multidisciplinary client service teams. While at Hodes, she initiated the firm's practices in diversity, health care, and public relations. Carol retired as a consultant who provided marketing support to professional health care associations and assisted not-for-profit organizations with executive recruitment.

Before you become a leader, success is all about growing yourself. When you become a leader, success is all about growing others.
—Jack Welch, (b. 1935),
chemical engineer, author, and
former CEO of General Electric

Relationship: former manager and current friend

Impact on my life:
Carol hired me in the Fort Lauderdale office of Bernard Hodes Group and was an unyielding advocate for my abilities and accomplishments throughout my twelve years with the company. I am proud to call Carol, my friend.

Dedra Paul is a human resources manager with almost thirty years of experience with corporate America. Her most recent position was as Employee Relations Manager at the Seminole Hard Rock Hotel and Casino, supporting more than 3,000 employees.

She is on the Diversity Committee at Greater Miami Society of Human Resources Management and on the Commission for Social Justice and Immigration for the Diocese of Southeast Florida. At Royal Caribbean Cruise Lines, Dedra was the diversity leader, developing, launching and managing diversity initiatives for a global vacation provider which employed over 20,000.

The quote below was written in Dedra's junior high school yearbook by one of her cousins. This phrase of brotherhood is always at the back of Dedra's mind and has formed the basis of her diversity work.

> There is a destiny that makes us brothers,
> none goes his way alone.
> All we send into the lives of others, comes back into our own.
> —Edwin Markham (1852—1940),
> American poet,
> Poet Laureate of Oregon from 1923 to 1931

Relationship: client and friend

Impact on my life:
Dedra was my first diversity services client at Royal Caribbean Cruise Lines. She helped me understand the role of human resources in an organization. We have maintained our friendship over time and distance.

Martha Ceja, Director and owner of The Outfit, provides uniform and branded solutions to local, regional and national corporate clients. Martha has extensive experience in retail, strategic sales, and marketing and communications. She spent over ten years as a Manager for Diversity & Inclusion Solutions at Bernard Hodes Group. Martha has over fifteen years of sales, project management, and marketing and communications experience. She has conducted diversity training sessions for recruiters around best practices in diversity recruitment. In her early years in the workforce, she worked as Director of Fund Distribution for United Way.

Martha holds a Bachelor of Science degree from San Jose State University and Master's degree in Business Administration from the University of Phoenix. Martha currently resides in the Sacramento area with her husband and two loving daughters, Erika and Sophia. You will often find her juggling work and the next track meet or speech and debate tournament for one of her daughters.

Do what you love and the money will come.

—Juan Carlos Ceja,
clothing manufacturer and Martha's husband

Relationship: staff/employee and friend

Impact on my life:
One of the best business decisions I ever made, was to hire Martha. She is brilliant and loyal, and we are friends for life.

Frank Scruggs litigates employment and commercial disputes, including class actions, and advises companies and executives regarding employment law compliance. He has a distinctive combination of experiences: litigator of complex business disputes, corporate and governmental policy-maker, and director of major corporations. Frank served as Secretary of Labor and Employment Security for the State of Florida.

Frank helps companies manage workplace and commercial risks. He uses counseling to help companies avoid litigation, and courtrooms, and negotiations to resolve disputes. He is a member of the Boards of Directors of SunTrust Banks, Inc. and Blue Cross Blue Shield of Florida, Inc., *Florida Blue*.

Proverbs 3:5-6
(KJV)
Trust in the LORD with all thine heart,
and lean not unto thine own understanding;
in all thy ways acknowledge Him,
and He shall direct thy paths.

Relationship: colleague

Impact on my life:
Early in my public speaking career, I met Frank—he was on the same program—at a diversity conference. He calmed me down backstage and gave good advice: "if you're not a *little* nervous you will be flat and probably boring."

Michael Wheeler, Global Lead, Diversity and Inclusion Strategy and Business Insights at Merck. He has over two decades of experience working with government, not-for-profits and Fortune 500 companies. He was a Program Director and Research Associate for The Conference Board where he launched their first executive Council on Workforce Diversity, their Annual Diversity Conference and Workshops, and their diversity research area of expertise. He has written and published extensively on the topic of diversity, been cited in newspapers around the world and appeared on television and radio (including Larry King Live). His articles and research include the first special sections on diversity in both Harvard Business Review and Business Week. He holds his undergraduate degree from the California State University and his graduate degree from Milano School of International Affairs, Management, and Urban Policy of The New School University.

Every great dream begins with a dreamer. Always remember, you have within you the strength, the patience, and the passion to reach for the stars to change the world.
—Harriet Tubman (1820—1913),
abolitionist, nurse, and spy,
she led hundreds of slaves to freedom, along the Underground Railroad

Tubman is slated to become the first African-American on U.S. Currency: the $20 bill. Already called a "Tubman" by some.

Relationship: colleague

Impact on my life:
In his role with The Conference Board, he put me on the program as a speaker for this influential institution, which helped open doors to consultation assignments with various organizations and corporations. Michael is a friend of a dear friend (Alexandra Bassil) and therefore, my friend too.

Lisa P. Gaynier, founder of the leadership consulting firm, creativechange.biz, Lisa Gaynier joined Cleveland State as director of the nation's only Master's program in Diversity Management (MA-DMP) in 2006. The MA-DMP is a weekend executive MBA-style program, for mid-career adults that *develops culturally competent leaders for a global economy.* A native of *Hawai'i,* Gaynier is of Asian/ Pacific Island and European descent. She is the author of an *award-winning multi-cultural cookbook,* an *award-winning academic paper on the development of culturally competent leaders,* in addition to papers on mediation and organization effectiveness.

Gaynier is involved in community redevelopment and revitalization projects, served on the Board of the Northern Ohio Minority Supplier Development Council and is former board chair of the Cleveland Mediation Center. She lives in Cleveland Heights, OH with her life partner, Michael.

> The peace I am thinking of, is the dance of an open mind
> when it engages another equally open one.
> —Toni Morrison (b.1931), author,
> noted for her examination of the black female experience in
> the U.S.A.,
> awarded the Nobel Prize for Literature, 1993

Relationship: colleague and friend

Impact on my life:
I never imagined I would be a participant at a meeting held at the United Nations. Not only did I attend, I met Lisa. I so admire her positive outlook on life and work.

Virgie Nell (Matthews) Merritt Dowdell, was born December 11, 1923, in Grady AL, Crenshaw County. She was the fourth child of eleven, born to Valeria Posey and Will Matthews. She married my father, Henry W. Merritt, whom she had known from childhood, on Pearl Harbor Day, December 7, 1941; and they were married for nineteen years. Mom-a-dear held various jobs in dietary at hospitals in Cleveland and New Jersey. She retired from the Cleveland Public Schools at age seventy-five. She currently lives in Cleveland, OH and has lived in Texas, Missouri, Michigan and New Jersey. She is always ready for new experiences and travel. Mom-a-dear draws comfort from her religion—Baptist; and she particularly loves this Bible verse—

Matthew 3:17
(KJV)

And lo, a voice from heaven, saying,
This is my beloved Son, in whom I am well pleased.

Relationship: mother and friend

Impact on my life:
Her wisdom is eternal and ever present in my life. My mother also loves poetry. As a young student at Helicon High School, she had to memorize this poem (an excerpt):

Trees

I think that I shall never see
A poem lovely as a tree.

A tree that looks at God all day,
And lifts her leafy arms to pray.

Poems are made by fools like me,
But only God can make a tree.

—Joyce Kilmer (1886—1918), poet and WW I hero,
awarded the Croix de Guerre (Cross of War)
by the French Republic

My mother's advice for me and my brothers: "you must work for whatever you get." And her sage advice to "just remember, you were looking for a job when you got this one, and you'll be looking for a job when you leave," so don't despair, you can always find another. That advice helped me move on, with enthusiasm, from one job to another as I followed my husband and his career around the country; and allowed me to overcome the trauma of "downsizing" in 2010.

Iran S. Cummings worked as a District Sales Manager for Chevrolet and for General Motors for thirty-four years, now retired. He started out at Chevrolet as a contract employee, then moved on to technician at GM Truck and Bus, and then as a customer service representative in the Buick Dealer Center and finally for the last twenty-five years as a District Sales Manager for Buick, GMC and Cadillac, and Chevrolet.

Prior to his years with General Motors, he worked for Wyeth Labs as a pharmaceutical representative and as a consultant with Professional Budget Plan. He also was a Distributive Education student teacher at Collingwood High School. He graduated from Akron University with a B.S. in Education and spent his first two years of college at Fisk University. Iran has an M.B.A. from the University of Detroit and an A.S. in Robotics from Macomb Community College.

As a three-letter high school athlete, Iran has continued his passionate participation in sports: volleyball, billiards, softball, bowling and golf. He is treasured by his wife, Annette, daughter Tahlia, step-children, Michael and Angela and all the grandchildren.

Relationship: husband

Impact on my life:
The best person I know to discuss ideas with and develop a plan of action. His sense of humor brings "joy" to my life.

Iran's inspiration for the journey:

The Teaching of Tecumseh
(Excerpt)

Live your life that the fear of death can never enter your heart.

Love your life, perfect your life, and beautify all things in your life.
Seek to make your life long and of service to your people.

When your time comes to die, be not like those whose hearts are filled with fear of death, so that when their time comes they weep and pray for a little more time to live their lives over again in a different way.

Sing your death song, and die like a hero going home.

—Tecumseh (1768—1813),
Shawnee, Native American Chief, orator,
and military leader

What lies before us and what lies behind us are simple matters compared to what lies within us.

—Ralph Waldo Emerson (1803—1882),
lecturer, poet, and essayist

We must pay the world for the space we take.

—Modjeska Monteith Simkins (1899—1992),
leader in African American public health, social reform,
and the Civil Rights movement in South Carolina

Modjeska Monteith Simkins lived in Columbia, SC. She is legendary in this area of the South. Long-time residents still talk about her dedication, outspokenness and perseverance. Her former home is now used as a meeting place and training facility for progressive action.

Chapter 10.

PARTING WORDS AND LESSONS

The trouble with using experience as a guide is that the final exam comes first and then the lesson.
—Anonymous

Count your blessings, not your crosses,
Count your gains, not your losses.
Count your joys instead of your woes,
Count your friends instead of your foes.
Count your health, not your wealth.

—Old Proverb

Former Senator Bill Bradley opened his speech at the Washington Speakers Bureau with this quote:

The two most important days of your life:
when you are born and when you know why.

—Mark Twain (1835—1910),
pseudonym of Samuel L. Clemens,
humorist, journalist, lecturer and novelist

When I heard this quote—it had a profound impact on me. At the time, I did not know that Mark Twain said it originally. Since then, I have often used this quote to close or open a speech.

Life is not measured by the number of breaths we take, but by the moments that take our breath away.

—Anonymous

We ought to hear at least one little song every day,

read a good poem,

see a first rate painting, and,

if possible, speak a few sensible words.

—Johann Wolfgang von Goethe (1749—1832),
German poet, playwright, novelist, and scientist

Psalm 90:10 (KJV)

The days of our years *are* threescore years and ten;
and if by reason of strength *they be* fourscore years,
yet *is* their strength labour and sorrow,
for it is soon cut off, and we fly away.

We are here for only a short time, so if we can discover our purpose
or mission in life, we are one of the lucky ones.

ACKNOWLEDGEMENTS

For encouraging me to write this book
Iran Cummings, my husband.
Carol Barber, editor, booster and friend.

For my life: thanks to my family
Mom-a-dear, Daddy, Will Henry, LaDon, Mamma Laura, Pa Henry, Aunt Sylvia, Michael (Renetta), Angela (Timonthy) and Tahlia.

For my love of reading:
Mamma Laura, Aunt Sylvia and Mom-a-dear.

For our future: be fearless!
Donte, Corey, Courtney, Trevor, Simone, LaNez and JaRell. Aujinae, Niza, Trace, Jordan, Jeremiah, Lennox, Jaden, Cali and one on the way.

My gratitude forever to my darling husband, Iran, for his support of me, my goals and decisions...no matter what.

My feet's is tired, but my soul is rested.
—Woman in the Montgomery Bus Boycott

45th John F. Kennedy High School
Reunion, Cleveland, OH
My husband, Iran's Class of 1969

Thanks *be* unto God for His unspeakable gift.

2 Corinthians 9:15 (KJV)

ABOUT THE AUTHOR

Annette Merritt Cummings, founder and managing partner of Cummings and Company LLC, has over thirty years of experience in marketing and communications with leading U.S. companies and non-profits, including DuPont, Gannett, and the National Board for Professional Teaching Standards and the Department of Defense. During her advertising and public relations career, clients have included U.S. Army Recruiting Command, Ford Motor Company, General Motors, and The Ohio State University Athletics.

Prior to her retirement as Vice President and National Director of Diversity Services for Bernard Hodes Group, she advised clients on diversity branding, communications, recruitment and retention strategies for over twelve years. Annette served as a featured speaker and conducted numerous workshops and training sessions for many Federal agencies and Fortune 500 corporations. She was a contributing author to the book, *On Staffing, Advice and Perspectives* from *HR Leaders*. Annette's most recent workshop was, *"The Best of Times, The Worst of Times," Cross-Cultural Communications* for the Association of Training and Development (ASTD) South Carolina Midlands Chapter.

Based on her personal interest in history and the arts, Annette is a member of the National Trust for Historic Preservation, Historic Columbia, Columbia Museum of Art and Americans for the Arts. She also volunteers at Historic Columbia and previously served as co-chair of membership for the American Association of University Women, South Carolina (AAUW-SC) and is a lifelong member of the Public Relations Society of America. Annette is an avid reader and belongs to the Richland County Library Sandhills Branch Thursday Book Club, enjoys historic travel, and the visual and performing arts. She recently joined in weekly Bible Study Fellowship sessions. She is a Civil War history buff and a devoted fan of the Cleveland Browns. Her husband, Iran, worked as a General Motors district sales manager and is a gifted gardener and gourmet cook. Combined they have three children: Michael, Angela and Tahlia, seven grandchildren, and eight great-grands.

TO CONTACT THE AUTHOR

Annette Merritt Cummings is available for motivational speaking engagements or workshops on: cultural competence, diversity, and inclusion. She is also available for executive coaching and briefings on communication with diverse audiences, marketing and public relations strategies. Annette welcomes the opportunity to speak to book clubs and community groups.

Author's email:
aicummings@msn.com

Printed in the United States
By Bookmasters